T0131860

Knowing the Best of
Princess Diana

Written and Illustrated by:
Mariagorretti E.O. Noble

To order additional copies of this book, contact:
Xlibris
844-714-8691
www.Xlibris.com
Orders@Xlibris.com

ISBN: Softcover   978-1-6698-0392-8
        Hardcover   978-1-6698-0393-5
        EBook   978-1-6698-0394-2

Print information available on the last page

Rev. date: 05/24/2022

Knowing the Best of
Princess Diana

Written and Illustrated by:
Mariagorretti E.O. Noble

Table of Contents

1.Such a sudden-Lady Diana

Such a wonderful born English child, that the whole world loved so much. I have never seen such a woman in my life. Such a sudden she grew up, and participated in so many activities while attending school. Such a sudden, she finished school, and became an assistant teacher and a nanny at the time. I am also an assistant teacher. Imagine such a wonderful noble child working so hard to make a living regardless. All of a sudden, the world chose her as one of the most beautiful women that would suit Prince Charles besides other girls. Such a sudden she married Prince Charles. I looked at her, and I said to myself that this was a match made in heaven. As I watched Diana during the wedding, she looked up in the sky, and looked around breathing in, and out, the sweet fresh air, she smiled, in her mind thinking that this day was like an unbelievable dream. At the same time, I myself felt the same. Such a sudden she became pregnant, giving birth to her first son, William, and such a sudden she gave birth to her second son, Harry. The children would then grow up to attend prestigious schools and would become the future King, and Future Duke of England.

A GIFT TO Diana

Lady Di's,

Crown.

Such a sudden Diana would become the future Queen, in which the whole world was expecting that she would be one day. Such a sudden the marriage between Prince Charles, and Lady Diana went sour and she chose to become the Queen of hearts instead. In this case, I wonder, with dismay why would she say something that might hurt her royalty. Oh, such a wonderful human being. It is hard to find such a beautiful, and glamorous lady with royalty, who devotes herself to the poor and sick people, and even those with AIDS, leprosy, and all kinds of diseases. Infact, she is such an outstanding human being who tries so hard to confront those in need, by making the public aware of all the problems that face the world including the hungry and third world countries. She especially has founded charities to help those who are not fortunate, sick and needy. All of her clothing, hats and shoes that she wore were donated and auctioned off to charity because of her instinct to care for those who were less fortunate. In fact, everything fits her and she is a walking beauty that will never fade.

Everything that she touches leaves a sign of love, and she truly touched the world making this place to feel special. Frankly, everything happened so suddenly in her life. Such a sudden she befriended a man that gave her what she was looking for something called love, and she enjoyed it very much. Such a sudden, "Oh my God!" she died a sudden death which the whole world mourned her death showing their regards with flowers from all over the world, with all kinds of colors. The flower is also a path of her life. Imagine everywhere she goes, there are flowers in her hand given to her by the people, who are waiting, watching her, and expressing their love to her. Even the stars in the sky love her byexuding her beauty, grace and style. It was such a sudden everything around her happened such a sudden. Because of her death, I myself was unable to watch T.V for almost 6 months. My whole body was in such a shock, and I prayed to God to help me out. Such a sudden, I can't believe it! Such a sudden the world turned upside down for Lady Diana. Such a sudden, the world buried Lady Diana and such a sudden the world missed her forever. Oh, Lady Diana, Lady Diana, Why such a sudden?

2.Living in a Palace

Living in a palace is like living in an exciting world where you can find anything you ever wanted and needed. Many different people would travel from all over the world to visit the King, Queen, Prince and Princess. They would come to see all the exciting things in the palace.When I look up at the palace, I wonder how they came up with the word King, Queen, Prince and Princess. Then there came a castle, which was built with stone, marble, cement and brick. Some are built within the river, so as to prevent the enemy from invading. But I see all of this, as living in a wonderful world. It is a world in which you cannot penetrate very easily. I can see that everything in a palace looks very special to the eyes of the world. The nannies and the butlers even live in the palace, too! And a palace is filled with so many precious things, and sometimes I imagine how they eat, dress and sleep. And I say to myself: "Are they not the same person as we are?"

I think of her not living anymore. But I think of her still living and invisible. Sometimes I think that she could have been alive by now if only she remained in the palace. But uncertainty is always a case. Our eyes are not always open when we are asleep, and we think that we can foresee the future, but we can't see clearly as we may have thought. In my opinion, the world is filled with probabilities, certainties and uncertainties. But remember that we always have to ask God to help us to see what we can't see in our lives. But this incident could have been prevented by God. I wonder how her spirit wanders. I wonder if her spirit sees all that took place after she died. I know that she will be happy to see that everything is working fine. I know she will be watching her children in spirit, just like she did while she was living. I know that she worked very diligently for everyone, both the poor and rich. I know that she would have wished to live a long life as to help the world to become a better place. She chose to be the Queen of hearts, but also simultaneously, the people chose her to be the Queen of all Queens. As you can see, when she passed away the world wondered, cried and united for her. The earth moved for her. The stars worshiped her, including the moon, which gleamed even brighter for that moment. People of the world wondered and wondered all day long and all night long. The whole world wished that she were alive so that they could have given her flowers, but she wasn't alive. So they kept on throwing flowers upon flowers at her house and anywhere that they had seen her, until the flowers became scarce for some time. When she died, I was filled with imagination and could not understand how such a thing could happen to Lady Diana. I think it was such a loss to the world. Oh God! I wished that this; would have never happened. I wonder and think and I wish that the whole world would remember and pray for her forever.

Diana was a woman of elegance, grace and class. Everything that she went through; from growing up to her highly publicized marriage and life came in the form of an ocean. Sometimes calm and sometimes rough. At times she wondered how her problems could be solved. Day by day, night by night she thought of ways to come to terms with her problems, but it always seemed that there was no way out. As far as being a woman, is concerned, women as a whole have no choice when living with a man. They lose some of their rights. And when you try to claim your right, then it becomes something abominable, sometimes you cry and sometimes you laugh. Next you see yourself as being trapped, tied up and unable to escape. Again you felt astonished and ask yourself;

wasn't this the paradise that you were living in? And you think and think but there were no answers when it comes to manhood. As for some women, every other week is beat up time. You called friends and your relations but there still was no change after a while. Then your problem would continue to progress in the form of verbal abuse, which often tends to result in a cruel manner. Sometimes every move you make becomes a problem and you are not allowed to breathe the fresh air. cry and sometimes you laugh. Next you see yourself as being trapped, tied up and unable to escape. Again you felt astonished and you ask yourself wasn't this the paradise that were living in? And you think and think but there were no answers when it comes to manhood. As for some women, every other week is beat up time. You called friends and your relations but there still was no change after a while. Then your problem would continue to progress in the form of verbal abuse, which often tends to result in a cruel manner. Sometimes every move you make becomes a problem and you are not allowed to breathe the fresh air.

In fact, there is nothing that you could do that would please some men but in some cases there are some women who are lucky to have everything surrounding them especially love which is the main reason for getting married. In fact, every woman is in need of help when it comes to their marriage. For example, when I went to Mass on one Sunday afternoon, there was snow all over the city like about five inches and it was very cold that day. I had to decide whether that Sunday, if I should go to church or not. At that time the Mass was already over and there was nobody in the church, but due to the Holy Spirit, I was moved to attend no matter what and to show my reverence and to pray to God, Almighty that particular Sunday. I was persuaded by the overwhelming divinity of the Holy Spirit to stay and pray. Well, nevertheless, I stayed and said my prayers even though the lights were turned off. Since my faith was very strong in God, I did not attain any fear at all. Then I went in and knelt down before God, and so as I was praying, I heard a sound; it was a young lady who had just walked inside the church and sat down a couple pews behind me. As she knelt down, I heard some sounds that kept on interrupting my prayers. It sounded like she had a cold. Well, I thought to myself that I might as well leave the church because she was making all sorts of sounds. In fact, as I was about to get up from the pew to walk out of the church, I felt the Holy Spirit, again, spiritually telling me not to leave this woman alone in the church without speaking to her. I asked myself "Why me?"

At the same time there was a family that had already been in the church before I came in and they had left without saying any word to console her. On that, I wondered and I felt more sympathetic and I asked myself again, "Why me?" So with the force of the Holy Spirit, I was able to walk up straight to her. As I took one step I halted, two steps I halted, and then three steps later I said to myself, I have to speak to her or I will remain guilty for the rest of my life for not trying to help her. At the same time I wondered how she would respond if I said hello to her but the Holy Spirit, kept urging me to go over to her. Then finally, I opened my mouth without any fear and said to her, "Are you okay" and she replied, "Yes, I am", with a faint voice and with tears all over her face as she turned around to respond to me. I tried to get a sense of what she was going through by randomly asking her questions and she said that she was having relationship problems as she tried to wipe off her tears that were running down her cheeks. Then I said to her to stop crying as she turned around to look at me. Well, I said to her, "I know what you are going through. Every once in a while, we as a human beings do go through certain difficulties." After that I told her that she did the right thing by coming to the right place in search of God, and that you should feel good about yourself, because heavenly Father is the one who sent you here to get some help and also that God was so great and worked in mysterious ways, that you remembered to come to him and for that matter your problems have been solved. The Angel of the Lord was with you and would always guide you whatever your problem might be. As I was speaking to her I felt the Holy Spirit within me, and the tears were about to run out of my eyes and I wiped it off gently because her problem had overwhelmed me as if it were my own problem. But at the same time, I felt very blissful and satisfied that I had done what God had sent me to do which was to help the lady and reassure her of the heavenly Father's love that he had for her.

As strange as it can be God works or helps people through different ways without us noticing that God has sent one of his angels so many times in order to help us through our difficulties no matter what. At the time, I finished speaking to her, she felt relieved and happy for the moment. She responded to me "Goodbye" and I too waved my hand and said goodbye to her, as I departed from the church. On the contrary to that I felt like a bird that was released from captivity while my imagination was filled with so many questions and answers, such as "Could it be that I was sent to go to Church because of her?" In fact, I tried to figure out why I left my apartment under such a snowy and very cold day throughout that day, but it came to me that no matter how bad the weather was that day my strong faith and belief in God and the Holy Spirit would continue to guide and watch over me. I as a person believe in God so greatly and I also love my fellow human beings whether they love me or not. And this is why I thought that God, almighty sent me as a representative of an Angel of the Lord to rescue this lady from agony. This example about this particular woman that I met at the church, reflects to Princess Diana's life and to every other woman that undergoes the bombardment or maltreatment of everyday marriages.

Diana was destined for royalty and to live in paradise but in that paradise that she lived in, was like a mountain surrounded by butterflies during the spring season, and on that there came the heavy rain that disturbed the butterflies from flying for a while. Nevertheless, Diana was unable to enjoy her paradise after the storm because of the manipulators. But still the ambitious Diana's beauty glowed like the morning sunshine and as the day goes by, the sun glowed stronger and stronger. Diana's essence glowed stronger and stronger in every aspects of life. Even though her marriage never got better, she learned how to believe in herself and to continue to move on. Diana never allowed the strong wind to push her down, no matter how hard the wind continued to blow. She always held herself up firm.

Again, some women sometimes are wrapped up with the fear of whether to leave their husband or to stay especially when children are involved. It is the most difficult decision to make. In this type of case, to go forwards is not good and to go backwards is not good either. On the other hand, as far as some women are concerned they have no choice but to live in the world of confusion. As for Diana, she also lived in the world of uncertainty. Diana portrays every woman; poor or rich, she never got tired of trying to unfold herself so many times from her problems in order to be happy. She never liked the notion of divorce because from what I understood, she did not want her marriage to be over. Diana felt that her life would be publicly displayed and dramatized by the media. Symbolically, marriage is like a parcel that is all tied up. You have no idea what is in it or whether it is fragile, which requires that you have to handle it with care. And you may also imagine whether the object inside may be good or bad.

Relationships as in today's society, as a result of being a woman, you may tend to develop stress and sometimes headaches that may come and go; due to your mind not being at rest. When you go in to the bedroom to lie down on the nice and comfortable bed made for two but it will turn out as if somebody dropped a ton of gravel on top of it. Instead, of the bed being comfortable, it becomes uncomfortable. You toss around in the bed because you can't sleep and you notice that your spouse has occupied more than half of the bed while you struggle for some space so that you don't fall off from the bed. Anyways, since your partner lacks communication skills, you have no other choice than to talk to him whether he likes it or not. Some of us, women get very weak and just can't let go for a while what we feel or have in mind, which leads us to cry like there is no tomorrow. But for some women "after all tomorrow is another day". But even though you tried to get through to him, the result of response could be so slim until he decides to listen to you.Women in general need to be treated properly, with love and care and most of all to give them equal rights. For example, in some parts of the world women are not allowed to dress certain ways or to have an education or to join in the mist of other men, while they are talking or holding a meeting or even to take your advice even though the advice might be fruitful. In some parts of the world, you have the ability for equal rights. Some men can do whatever they want to do at any time, but to some men; women can't. And some men think that women should and therefore must abide by their rules. Well, this is very unfair to women.

Another example about Diana's way of life is that love is portrayed as an essence. When in fact, love is a sham. You are never satisfied by the one you supposedly love. We mobilize from one relationship to another using, expressing, exaggerating that word love, wasting our time thinking that, that person is the one for us when in fact, we tire for the one that we are with. With a quest to find someone that makes us tingly and light in the head. There is no one person, and that is why we cheat and lust because we are not satisfied with our present relationship. We get weak in the knees and can hardly speak but when in fact we are just feeling not that we are in love. We crave as humans to be tempted to find someone more exciting that we loose control of what we see. Love is nothing more than a word used to tie us down from wanting to believe that there will not only be one person that you want to spend the rest of your life with but others that you feel and want to share your time with in this world and not being constricted to that one person.

Diana, you are the flower that glows when the sun shines and that everyone should smell it. Princess Diana's wedding celebration is like a pool of diamonds that everyone adores and therefore they are eager to be around her since she brings so much joy. Her wedding gown was like no other wedding dress, it was the only one in the whole world. Imagine having such a wedding that made the whole world to listen, cry, sing and dance. The seamstress concocted an extraordinary and exquisite wedding gown that also made her to look more gorgeous than she had ever looked. The crown that she wore on her head followed by a veil, had already proclaimed her the Princess of the people. Her veil was so long that when it was measured it could be up to 25 feet long in estimate. There was a lot of traditional wedding preparations, which included Diana and Charles getting together and learning more about each other and one another's families. And they both had to learn each other and how to live together like a loving couple who were destined to be Queen and King of England.The jewelry that Diana wore bore the treasures of exquisite semi-preciouss tones with diamonds as bright as her smile that will last forever in the eyes of the people. The crowd appeared to grow more and more weary, gradually awaiting for Diana's arrival and anxious to see her and how beautiful she looked that day. The firecrackers sounded like thunder bolts crashing in the sky. As Princess Diana of Wales emerged from the church, the whole world watched waiting to get a glance and to be enchanted by the

Princess' beauty that day. It was just like a fairy tale story but that fairy tale ended up in divorce. Indeed, it was a great dream that came true because it made Diana known to the whole world and thus she would continue to play an important role in the peoples' life. Being too young has a lot to do with marriage. That is it takes a lot of courage, patience, and understanding the facts of marriage.

4.Living With the Pain Within

Diana's relationship with Charles was only love on one side. It was a kind of love that Diana never expected. Moreover, Diana was carried a way by the unpredictable phases of marriage. In any event, she thought it was a relationship that was going to last. "Forever I and Charles are in this love together," said Diana. Well, at last it became a menace in the dark room, and during the daylight it was so deceitful to the world for sometime.

Diana was known as the lady that wanted to dance, who wanted to spend time with her sons, William and Harry and she was even very active and participated in charitable causes in her spare time. And as I may say, the world may never know what we as the universe have missed. If I may add, She could have been one of the angels or even a saint, one may never know. The fantasy that Diana has found has come to be real at last. Diana was a very fantastic and articulate lady. She was a lady born to be wise and charming, with an everlasting beauty that was surrounded by the brightness of diamonds. Diana was a diamond that lasted forever, and that could never be compared to any other women. She was one of a kind, never fake and she had a smile as lustrous as a diamond. I can say that some people did not get a chance to really learn about Diana's life but the world may understand the notion that all that glitters is not gold. With respect to Diana, in this aspect, in her own case, all that glitters may turn out to be gold. Diana was the mirror for all women and her spirit was unbreakable.

What about all the love? What about all the happiness? What about all the dreams? What about all the jewelry? What about all the love that brought them together. What about all those kisses? What about all her beauty that she had? Her smile sparkled whenever she opened her mouth.Why can't Charles see such an elegant woman and give her what she wants all the time? What went wrong with the husband not seeing her clearly? What more could he want besides Diana? Which woman distracted Charles from Diana? Is it really another woman, or has he lost the love that he had for Diana? It's just like a love that was gone with the breeze with no apparent exclamation. Princess Diana is like a sunset to every woman, by which when a sunflower opens it's petals, it faces towards the sun and becomes comfortable. Therefore, the sun is able to accommodate and to provide such a profound love, peace, courage, and stamina to the sunflower. Diana paved the way for women by giving them the strength needed to follow their heart. In this aspect, women should learn how to be strong like her and also to have self-confidence, self-image, and simplicity. "Life is a stage" and so was Diana's life by which she had to learn the hardships and pleasures that came with it. Once stated, some are born great, some achieve greatness, and some greatness are entrusted upon them. In Diana's case, she was born great, she was born to achieve greatness and also her greatness was entrusted upon her at the same time. In any event, she will always remain an inspiration to every human being especially women. The world will never forget her.

Some women in general seem to have the idea that being in love is all in all everything, but they have not gotten the concept of the mainstream that comes with love, which also includes understanding the whole concept of what marriage is really all about. All over the world, no matter what the tradition or how much it may cost, or if the transition of marriage came crashing down in a matter of a week, month, or a year the music that goes with the marriage also crashes the marriage. Sometimes marriage is like a beautiful dream that comes true, but sometimes it suddenly becomes a nightmare. Some men only want to take control of women by telling them to change their behavior, and constantly telling them what to do. At this moment the love has gone astray, and thus the woman has nothing to do but to take it or leave it.

Marriage, is like a full moon, that comes in a circle of phases during which may last months or even years. But like the full moon, marriage can tend to be loving and caring and at times it may end up in disappointment. When the moon's light begins to dimmer off in the night it can become dark and unknown. As a matter of fact, marriage is like a full moon that is at times unknown.

5.Diana's Perception on War

Diana believes that war is a disruption of humanity and a destruction of ones' life, soul, and spirit. She contested so much about war by traveling to so many countries. She believed that everything could be worked out diplomatically through amicable discussions. She understands war to be a very complex decision but it is not the best resort to take. She has the dedication, and believes in compassion for other human beings. She also has the vision of peaceful resolution rather than war. Diana believed that the conversion of war into peace would make a great difference in the world. By educating under developed, third world countries and by teaching the children about peace we could pave the way to understanding the overall benefits of peaceful resolutions. By all means, she would like each and every country in the world; whether it is a super power or third world country to play an important role on collaborating and working together for peace. Diana's act of kindness towards the world sets up an example to the world that if she can profess the ethics of peace and to impact the world with her words; then peace is achievable in any case. During Diana's mission for peace, she gave several speeches on world peace, which should not be ignored any way. No one has the authority to destroy anyone, because God created everyone equal. Her campaigning fight against war is something that the world will never forget. Thus, pledging for peace of all nations was what Diana wanted.

6.Diana On Relationship

Lady Diana the Princess of Wales embodied a profound beauty that was unquenchable for anybody. Whenever I sit down, I think about her standing in a large crowd like whales swimming high in the middle of theocean, and looking, so as you, Princess of Wales.

As for marriage, it is an implication and a disruption of life. A new you and a new world all together. It has level A, B, and C. Sometimes unimaginable as it may be. But of course it is a full moon. A full moon with an unknown label that comes with pleasures and treasures. A full moon that comes with many patterns of love. A full moon is good for some and bad for others. Diana thought that the journey of love would be the best thing to encounter. For example, the quest for love is a very rocky road for some people. At first, love was like a dream that came true. In this case, I have the notion that love is like spring water that is always crystal clear, but the moment more than one person gets in the middle of the stream, some dirty particles like dead leaves or other objects surfaces up until every one has deserted from the area and allows it to settle back again. So this is how love walked its way into everyone's life. The quest for love turns to sugar in many cases.

Maltreatment of Princess Diana, which causes maladjustment to her for some time. As her marriage started to crumble, the mother-in-law, never pardoned her as a young princess or consoled her in order to make the marriage work. Instead, she encouraged divorce, which in turn helped to shatter the little hope that she had all along as she waited to hear the good news from the Queen, which never came. As she hid away from the news media, her mind wonders as she tries to discover her identity. Again her heart hardened. Camilla Parker Bowls never cared about Diana's marriage, and her children, and the consequences that lay ahead. Camilla, in I my view, is a self-centered person. She took away the most precious gift from Diana and left her in the wilderness to wander like a sheep without a shepherd. In any event, Diana was able to find afew men who gave her the love and few who betrayed her and many who came to her rescue. While her life was uplifted again. She became involved in so many different activities, which paved her way to become a bright and shining star that the whole world would never forget; Diana was like a lightening bolt.

Dodi Al Fayed

Passionate with integrity, she touched everyone that she loved. Diana was an icon of the world, the one and only woman, who left a profound impact on many peoples lives. As Jesus said in the Bible to his people, "I come not to destroy the law and the prophet but to fulfill them." In this aspect, the world should know that Diana came to fulfill her duties as the mother of William and Harry, the future heirs to the throne of England and to become Princess of the people. In this case, people should not judge her for what they think about her based on the media's publicity but that they should see that she is a woman with extraordinary capabilities, who was sent by God to teach the world how to love and care for each other. And yet she was rejected by the few people, whom did not believe in her philosophy of how the world could be a better place without the use of land mines and war as a solution. She also addressed problems pertaining to bad marriages and issues of medical aides and extensive research to combat all kinds of diseases. In fact some people like me might think that she was like a prophet that was sent by God to save the world. But when she died suddenly, the whole world was totally in grief. I respect Diana, with that I leave you with one quote, "a mind is a terrible thing to waste" and as a matter of fact, Diana's mind is a terrible thing that the world has lost, and thank God that we are able to save a little bit of her.

7.Diamond

A diamond is forever and so is Princess Diana. Even though she is dead, she still lives in spirit. The way she looked, the way she changed her hairstyles inspired many people to mimic her style. Many people admired the way she walked majestically. Forever Princess Diana, your majesty, still lives on as a lady that was sent from the sky to her mother's womb.How wonderful you are Princess Diana. The day you were born was very exceptional. You are a representation for every woman whether they are beloved or abused.

Diana was known as the lady that helped out the whole world in time of need and in return the whole world thanked and loved her. The mother of the future King of England. Diana was a wise and perceptive woman. Diana, is still the Princess that still lives within so many people's hearts. And I say to you again, your majesty forever.

Diana's eyes are as blue as the sky. Her voice is as soft as a gentle wind. In her picture she looks very much alive. If you look at her very closely she shines like a diamond. When she wraps herself with a white towel in her room in the New York City hotel, then she appears like an angel, looking, and standing through the window.

Princess Diana as she is dancing the night away smiling the days away with such beautiful eyes, teeth, nose, lips, and exceptional hair styles. She dresses up with beautiful necklaces and clothes. She is as elegant as silk. The one and only Diana with no duplications of her. I wish I could see you again, I can't take my eyes off of your pictures. I wish I could talk to you. The world without Princess Diana is like a world without a single flower. She is a flower that the world wishes to smell. The beautiful flower that you can't resist. The shining Diana, I bow down for your majesty. A lady that was born to be wise. A lady that never missed her steps whenever she walked. A lady that had class, intelligence, and knowledge. Anywhere she went, the world respected the ground that she walked on. Diana portrayed herself as a woman of many talents with a sense of sophistication and class. Many people wanted to emulate her style. She was as kind as an angel, Diana is like a flower that the butterflies will miss forever. The birds of the world will never stop singing for Diana. The ocean will never stop being blue for Diana to swim in. The mountain will not get any higher than Diana. The ground that she steps on is still waiting for her footsteps. The world still turns and wishes for Diana to wake up.

Printed in the United States
by Baker & Taylor Publisher Services